50 Zodiac Chef Recipes

By: Kelly Johnson

Table of Contents

- Aries Fire-Grilled Lamb Chops
- Taurus Truffle Mac and Cheese
- Gemini Split Personality Tacos
- Cancer Creamy Crab Bisque
- Leo Roasted Golden Chicken
- Virgo Herb-Infused Quinoa Bowl
- Libra Balance Berry Tart
- Scorpio Dark Chocolate Chili
- Sagittarius Global Spice Stir-Fry
- Capricorn Mountain Mushroom Risotto
- Aquarius Electric Blue Smoothie
- Pisces Ocean Dream Sushi Roll
- Aries Sizzling Steak Skewers
- Taurus Honey-Glazed Short Ribs
- Gemini Yin Yang Spring Rolls
- Cancer Moonlight Lobster Bake
- Leo Sunburst Citrus Salmon

- Virgo Green Goddess Salad
- Libra Rosewater Pistachio Cake
- Scorpio Forbidden Black Rice Bowl
- Sagittarius Nomad's Naan Pizza
- Capricorn Goat Cheese Stuffed Peppers
- Aquarius Galactic Veggie Wrap
- Pisces Mermaid Ramen
- Aries Volcano Spaghetti
- Taurus Earthy Beetroot Risotto
- Gemini Dual-Flavor Donuts
- Cancer Starry Night Shrimp Scampi
- Leo Lion's Mane Burgers
- Virgo Perfectly Poached Eggs
- Libra Vanilla Lavender Latte
- Scorpio Red Velvet Lava Cake
- Sagittarius Coconut Curry Caravan
- Capricorn Root Vegetable Tart
- Aquarius Moonbeam Matcha Bowl
- Pisces Neptune's Paella

- Aries Bold BBQ Jackfruit
- Taurus Rustic Olive Bread
- Gemini Two-Tone Pasta Salad
- Cancer Creamy Clam Chowder
- Leo Golden Mango Sorbet
- Virgo Lemon Thyme Roasted Chicken
- Libra Dual-Chocolate Fondue
- Scorpio Crimson Beet Smoothie
- Sagittarius Moroccan Tagine Adventure
- Capricorn Stone Oven Flatbread
- Aquarius Starfruit Citrus Ceviche
- Pisces Dreamy Seafoam Cupcakes
- Aries Blazing Hot Wings
- Pisces Floating Fish Cakes

Aries Fire-Grilled Lamb Chops

Ingredients:

- 8 lamb chops
- 2 tbsp olive oil
- 4 cloves garlic, minced
- 1 tbsp fresh rosemary, chopped
- 1 tbsp fresh thyme, chopped
- 1 tsp smoked paprika
- Salt and black pepper to taste
- Lemon wedges (for serving)

Instructions:

1. Combine olive oil, garlic, rosemary, thyme, paprika, salt, and pepper in a bowl.
2. Rub the mixture all over the lamb chops and let them marinate for at least 30 minutes.
3. Preheat a grill or grill pan to high heat.
4. Sear the lamb chops for 3-4 minutes per side for medium-rare, or longer for desired doneness.
5. Let them rest for 5 minutes before serving with lemon wedges.

Taurus Truffle Mac and Cheese

Ingredients:

- 1 lb elbow macaroni
- 2 tbsp butter
- 2 tbsp flour
- 2 cups whole milk
- 1 cup heavy cream
- 2 cups sharp white cheddar, shredded
- 1 cup Gruyère cheese, shredded
- 2 tbsp truffle oil
- Salt and pepper to taste
- Fresh chives, chopped (optional)

Instructions:

1. Cook macaroni according to package instructions. Drain and set aside.
2. In a saucepan, melt butter over medium heat. Whisk in flour and cook for 1 minute.
3. Slowly add milk and cream, whisking constantly until thickened.
4. Stir in the cheeses until melted and smooth.
5. Add truffle oil, season with salt and pepper.
6. Combine with the cooked pasta. Garnish with chives and serve warm.

Gemini Split Personality Tacos

Ingredients:

- 1/2 lb ground beef
- 1/2 lb shredded rotisserie chicken
- 1 packet taco seasoning
- 1/2 cup water
- 8 small corn or flour tortillas
- 1 cup shredded lettuce
- 1 cup diced tomatoes
- 1/2 cup shredded cheese
- Sour cream, guacamole, salsa for topping

Instructions:

1. In one skillet, cook ground beef with half the taco seasoning and 1/4 cup water until browned.
2. In another skillet, heat chicken with the remaining seasoning and 1/4 cup water until warmed through.
3. Warm tortillas on a dry pan or in the oven.
4. Fill half the tortillas with beef and half with chicken.
5. Top with lettuce, tomatoes, cheese, and desired condiments.
6. Serve with both versions side-by-side for the full Gemini effect.

Cancer Creamy Crab Bisque

Ingredients:

- 2 tbsp butter
- 1 small onion, finely chopped
- 2 cloves garlic, minced
- 1/4 cup flour
- 2 cups seafood stock
- 1 cup heavy cream
- 1/2 cup white wine (optional)
- 1/2 tsp Old Bay seasoning
- 8 oz lump crab meat
- Salt and pepper to taste
- Chives or parsley for garnish

Instructions:

1. Melt butter in a pot over medium heat. Sauté onion and garlic until soft.
2. Stir in flour to make a roux and cook for 1-2 minutes.
3. Gradually whisk in seafood stock, followed by cream and wine.
4. Add Old Bay, salt, and pepper. Simmer for 10 minutes, stirring frequently.
5. Gently fold in crab meat and heat through without boiling.

6. Garnish with chives or parsley and serve hot.

Leo Roasted Golden Chicken

Ingredients:

- 1 whole chicken (about 4 lbs)
- 3 tbsp olive oil
- 1 tbsp turmeric
- 2 tsp smoked paprika
- 1 lemon, halved
- 6 cloves garlic
- Fresh rosemary and thyme sprigs
- Salt and pepper to taste

Instructions:

1. Preheat oven to 425°F (220°C).
2. Pat the chicken dry. Mix olive oil, turmeric, paprika, salt, and pepper. Rub all over the bird.
3. Stuff the cavity with lemon halves, garlic, and herbs.
4. Place in a roasting pan and roast for 1 hour to 1 hour 20 minutes, until golden and juices run clear.
5. Rest for 10 minutes before carving. Serve with roasted vegetables.

Virgo Herb-Infused Quinoa Bowl

Ingredients:

- 1 cup quinoa, rinsed
- 2 cups vegetable broth
- 1 tbsp olive oil
- 1/2 cup chopped cucumber
- 1/2 cup cherry tomatoes, halved
- 1/4 cup red onion, finely diced
- 1/4 cup fresh parsley and mint, chopped
- Juice of 1 lemon
- Salt and pepper to taste

Instructions:

1. Bring quinoa and broth to a boil, then simmer for 15 minutes. Fluff and let cool.
2. In a bowl, combine cooled quinoa, cucumber, tomatoes, onion, and herbs.
3. Drizzle with olive oil and lemon juice. Toss gently.
4. Chill before serving for best flavor.

Libra Balance Berry Tart

Ingredients:

- 1 pre-baked tart crust
- 1/2 cup cream cheese, softened
- 1/2 cup Greek yogurt
- 3 tbsp honey or maple syrup
- 1 tsp vanilla extract
- Mixed berries (blueberries, strawberries, raspberries)
- Mint for garnish

Instructions:

1. In a bowl, beat cream cheese, yogurt, honey, and vanilla until smooth.
2. Spread evenly over the tart crust.
3. Top with a symmetrical pattern of fresh berries.
4. Garnish with mint and chill for 30 minutes before slicing.

Scorpio Dark Chocolate Chili

Ingredients:

- 1 tbsp olive oil
- 1 lb ground beef or plant-based meat
- 1 onion, diced
- 2 cloves garlic, minced
- 1 can black beans
- 1 can crushed tomatoes
- 1 tbsp chili powder
- 1 tsp cumin
- 1/4 tsp cinnamon
- 2 squares (about 1 oz) dark chocolate
- Salt and pepper to taste

Instructions:

1. Heat oil in a pot and cook onion and garlic until soft.
2. Add ground meat and brown thoroughly.
3. Stir in beans, tomatoes, spices, and chocolate. Simmer 30 minutes.
4. Adjust seasoning. Serve with sour cream or jalapeños.

Sagittarius Global Spice Stir-Fry

Ingredients:

- 2 tbsp sesame oil
- 1 bell pepper, sliced
- 1 carrot, julienned
- 1/2 cup snap peas
- 1/2 cup mushrooms
- 1/2 block tofu or chicken, cubed
- 2 tbsp soy sauce
- 1 tbsp curry powder
- 1 tsp ginger paste
- Optional: sriracha or chili flakes

Instructions:

1. Heat oil in a large wok or pan. Sauté protein until golden.
2. Add vegetables and stir-fry 5–7 minutes.
3. Stir in soy sauce, curry, ginger, and optional spice.
4. Serve hot over jasmine rice or noodles.

Capricorn Mountain Mushroom Risotto

Ingredients:

- 1 tbsp olive oil
- 1/2 onion, minced
- 1 cup arborio rice
- 1/2 cup white wine (optional)
- 4 cups warm vegetable broth
- 1 cup mushrooms (shiitake, cremini), sliced
- 1/2 cup grated Parmesan
- 1 tbsp butter
- Fresh thyme or parsley

Instructions:

1. Heat oil in a pot. Sauté onion and mushrooms until tender.
2. Add rice, cook until edges look translucent.
3. Pour in wine, stir until absorbed.
4. Add broth one ladle at a time, stirring until creamy.
5. Finish with butter, cheese, and herbs. Serve warm.

Aquarius Electric Blue Smoothie

Ingredients:

- 1/2 frozen banana
- 1/2 cup pineapple
- 1/2 cup Greek yogurt
- 1/2 cup coconut water
- 1 tsp blue spirulina powder
- 1 tsp honey (optional)
- Ice cubes as needed

Instructions:

1. Combine all ingredients in a blender.
2. Blend until smooth and vibrant blue.
3. Pour into a glass and enjoy chilled.

Pisces Ocean Dream Sushi Roll

Ingredients:

- 1 cup sushi rice, cooked and seasoned
- 4 nori sheets
- 1/2 avocado, sliced
- 1/2 cucumber, julienned
- 4 imitation crab sticks or cooked shrimp
- Soy sauce, wasabi, and pickled ginger
- Optional: tobiko or spicy mayo

Instructions:

1. Lay a nori sheet on a bamboo mat.
2. Spread rice evenly, leaving 1-inch at the top bare.
3. Layer with avocado, cucumber, and seafood.
4. Roll tightly using the mat.
5. Slice into 6-8 pieces and serve with dipping sauces.

Aries Sizzling Steak Skewers

Ingredients:

- 1 lb sirloin steak, cut into cubes
- 1 red onion, cut into chunks
- 1 red bell pepper, cubed
- 2 tbsp soy sauce
- 1 tbsp Worcestershire sauce
- 1 tsp chili flakes
- 1 tbsp olive oil
- Skewers (soaked if wooden)

Instructions:

1. Marinate steak in sauces, chili flakes, and oil for 30 minutes.
2. Thread steak and veggies onto skewers.
3. Grill over medium-high heat 3–4 minutes per side.
4. Let rest before serving hot off the grill.

Taurus Honey-Glazed Short Ribs

Ingredients:

- 2 lbs beef short ribs
- 1/4 cup soy sauce
- 2 tbsp honey
- 1 tbsp rice vinegar
- 4 cloves garlic, minced
- 1 tsp ginger, grated
- 1 tsp sesame oil
- Sesame seeds and green onions for garnish

Instructions:

1. Whisk soy, honey, vinegar, garlic, ginger, and sesame oil.
2. Pour over ribs and marinate at least 2 hours or overnight.
3. Bake at 325°F (165°C) covered for 2.5 hours.
4. Uncover, broil 5–10 minutes to caramelize glaze.
5. Garnish and serve with rice or roasted veggies.

Gemini Yin Yang Spring Rolls

Ingredients:

- Rice paper wrappers
- 1/2 cup purple cabbage, shredded
- 1/2 cup carrot, julienned
- 1/2 avocado, sliced
- 1/2 mango, sliced
- Fresh mint and basil
- Cooked vermicelli noodles
- Peanut dipping sauce or hoisin sauce

Instructions:

1. Soak rice paper in warm water until soft.
2. Lay flat and layer noodles, cabbage, carrot, mango, avocado, and herbs.
3. Fold and roll tightly like a burrito.
4. Slice in half for a visual yin-yang display.
5. Dip and devour.

Cancer Moonlight Lobster Bake

Ingredients:

- 2 lobster tails, halved
- 2 ears of corn, cut into thirds
- 1/2 lb baby potatoes
- 1/2 lb shrimp, peeled
- 4 cloves garlic, minced
- 1 lemon, sliced
- 1/4 cup butter, melted
- Fresh parsley, salt, pepper

Instructions:

1. Preheat oven to 400°F (200°C).
2. Toss all ingredients in melted butter, garlic, and seasoning.
3. Arrange in a foil-lined baking dish with lemon slices.
4. Cover with foil and bake for 25–30 minutes.
5. Serve under candlelight or stars.

Leo Sunburst Citrus Salmon

Ingredients:

- 2 salmon fillets
- Juice of 1 orange
- Juice of 1 lemon
- 1 tbsp honey
- 1 tsp Dijon mustard
- Salt, pepper, and thyme
- Orange and lemon zest for garnish

Instructions:

1. Mix citrus juices, honey, mustard, salt, pepper, and thyme.
2. Pour over salmon and marinate 15–30 minutes.
3. Bake at 375°F (190°C) for 12–15 minutes.
4. Garnish with zest and serve with a golden side like couscous.

Virgo Green Goddess Salad

Ingredients:

- 2 cups mixed greens (spinach, arugula, romaine)
- 1/2 avocado, cubed
- 1/2 cucumber, sliced
- 1/4 cup edamame
- 2 tbsp pumpkin seeds
- Dressing: 1/4 cup Greek yogurt, 1 tbsp olive oil, juice of 1 lemon, 1 tbsp chopped fresh herbs (parsley, basil, dill), salt and pepper

Instructions:

1. Whisk together dressing ingredients until smooth.
2. In a large bowl, combine all greens and toppings.
3. Drizzle dressing and toss gently.
4. Enjoy with a tall glass of infused water.

Libra Rosewater Pistachio Cake

Ingredients:

- 1 cup flour
- 1/2 cup ground pistachios
- 1/2 cup sugar
- 1/2 cup butter, softened
- 2 eggs
- 1/4 cup milk
- 1 tsp rosewater
- 1 tsp baking powder
- Pinch of salt
- Optional glaze: powdered sugar + rosewater + milk

Instructions:

1. Preheat oven to 350°F (175°C).
2. Cream butter and sugar. Add eggs, milk, rosewater.
3. Mix dry ingredients and combine with wet.
4. Pour into a greased loaf pan. Bake 30–35 minutes.
5. Glaze and garnish with crushed pistachios or edible flowers.

Scorpio Forbidden Black Rice Bowl

Ingredients:

- 1 cup black rice
- 2 cups water
- 1/2 avocado, sliced
- 1/4 cup roasted sweet potato cubes
- 1/4 cup sautéed mushrooms
- 1 boiled egg, halved
- Drizzle: soy sauce + sesame oil + chili paste

Instructions:

1. Cook black rice in water until tender (about 30 mins).
2. Arrange rice in a bowl. Top with all other ingredients.
3. Drizzle spicy sauce on top.
4. Serve warm and mysterious.

Sagittarius Nomad's Naan Pizza

Ingredients:

- 2 pieces naan bread
- 1/2 cup hummus or tomato sauce
- 1/2 cup shredded cheese (or vegan cheese)
- Toppings: olives, red onion, bell pepper, feta, sun-dried tomatoes
- Za'atar or sumac for garnish

Instructions:

1. Preheat oven to 400°F (200°C).
2. Spread sauce over naan. Add cheese and toppings.
3. Bake 10–12 minutes until crispy.
4. Sprinkle with spices and take a bite of adventure.

Capricorn Goat Cheese Stuffed Peppers

Ingredients:

- 4 small bell peppers, halved and seeded
- 1/2 cup goat cheese
- 2 tbsp chopped walnuts
- 1 tbsp honey
- 1 tsp thyme
- Salt and black pepper

Instructions:

1. Preheat oven to 375°F (190°C).
2. Mix goat cheese, honey, thyme, salt, and pepper. Stir in walnuts.
3. Spoon into pepper halves.
4. Bake for 15–20 minutes until softened and golden.
5. Serve as a grounded, hearty starter or side.

Aquarius Galactic Veggie Wrap

Ingredients:

- Spinach or rainbow chard wraps
- Hummus or cashew cream
- Roasted purple sweet potato slices
- Shredded red cabbage
- Spiralized golden beet
- Microgreens
- Edible glitter or crushed blue corn chips (optional)

Instructions:

1. Spread hummus on wrap.
2. Layer in colorful veggies like a constellation.
3. Roll tightly, slice, and sprinkle with magic.
4. Serve with a side of stardust salsa.

Pisces Mermaid Ramen

Ingredients:

- Blue spirulina rice noodles or ramen noodles
- 1 soft-boiled egg
- Bok choy, enoki mushrooms, and tofu
- Seaweed sheets and scallions
- Dashi or veggie broth with a splash of coconut milk
- A drop of spirulina or butterfly pea flower for ocean color

Instructions:

1. Simmer broth with flavor additions.
2. Cook noodles and prep toppings.
3. Pour broth into a deep bowl and layer ingredients.
4. Garnish with seaweed and a dreamy egg half.

Aries Volcano Spaghetti

Ingredients:

- Spaghetti pasta
- Fiery arrabbiata or chili tomato sauce
- Crumbled sausage or mushrooms
- Fresh basil and red pepper flakes
- Parmesan or plant-based cheese
- Roasted red bell pepper "lava" strips

Instructions:

1. Cook pasta until al dente.
2. Sauté protein and mix into fiery sauce.
3. Plate pasta in a peak shape and ladle sauce like erupting magma.
4. Top with molten cheese and a flash of chili.

Taurus Earthy Beetroot Risotto

Ingredients:

- 1 cup arborio rice
- 2 cooked beets, grated
- 1/2 onion, minced
- 4 cups vegetable broth, warmed
- 1/4 cup white wine (optional)
- Goat cheese and thyme for garnish

Instructions:

1. Sauté onion, then stir in rice.
2. Add wine (if using), then slowly ladle in broth, stirring constantly.
3. Midway, stir in beet.
4. Finish creamy, top with cheese and thyme.

Gemini Dual-Flavor Donuts

Ingredients:

- Classic yeast or baked donut base
- Half dipped in dark chocolate glaze
- Half dipped in lemon glaze
- Optional fillings: raspberry jam + vanilla custard
- Sprinkles split down the middle

Instructions:

1. Bake or fry donuts.
2. Cool, then coat each side with a different glaze.
3. Add dual fillings for bonus contrast.
4. Serve as twin treats with flair.

Cancer Starry Night Shrimp Scampi

Ingredients:

- Linguine or angel hair pasta
- 1/2 lb shrimp, peeled
- 3 cloves garlic, minced
- 1/4 cup white wine or lemon juice
- Butter and olive oil
- Fresh parsley and lemon zest
- Edible star confetti or sea salt flakes for garnish

Instructions:

1. Sauté garlic and shrimp in butter/oil until pink.
2. Add wine or lemon juice, reduce slightly.
3. Toss with cooked pasta and parsley.
4. Sprinkle with zest and serve under a constellation of garnish.

Leo Lion's Mane Burgers

Ingredients:

- Lion's mane mushrooms or your favorite mushroom blend
- Olive oil, garlic, soy sauce
- Brioche buns
- Arugula, caramelized onions, and aioli
- Optional: smoked gouda or vegan cheese

Instructions:

1. Sear mushrooms with garlic and soy until golden.
2. Assemble buns with arugula, mushrooms, onions, cheese, and sauce.
3. Serve like royalty—bold and juicy.

Virgo Perfectly Poached Eggs

Ingredients:

- Fresh eggs
- Vinegar (for poaching water)
- Toasted sourdough
- Sliced avocado, cherry tomatoes, and microgreens
- Sea salt, black pepper, and chili flakes

Instructions:

1. Poach eggs in simmering water with vinegar.
2. Top toast with avocado, egg, and fresh toppings.
3. Season simply and enjoy with quiet perfection.

Libra Vanilla Lavender Latte

Ingredients:

- 1 cup milk of choice (steamed)
- 1 shot espresso or strong brewed coffee
- 1/2 tsp vanilla extract
- 1/2 tsp dried lavender or lavender syrup
- Honey or sweetener to taste

Instructions:

1. Brew espresso and mix with vanilla and sweetener.
2. Steam milk with lavender until infused.
3. Pour milk over espresso, stir gently.
4. Top with a sprinkle of dried lavender for harmony.

Scorpio Red Velvet Lava Cake

Ingredients:

- 1/2 cup dark chocolate chips
- 1/4 cup butter
- 1/4 cup sugar
- 2 eggs
- 1/4 cup flour
- Red food coloring or beet powder
- Pinch of espresso powder (optional)

Instructions:

1. Melt chocolate and butter. Whisk in sugar and eggs.
2. Fold in flour and coloring.
3. Pour into greased ramekins.
4. Bake at 425°F (220°C) for 10–12 minutes—outside firm, center molten.
5. Serve with ice cream and a smoldering stare.

Sagittarius Coconut Curry Caravan

Ingredients:

- Coconut milk
- Chickpeas or chicken
- Curry paste (red or yellow)
- Sweet potato, bell pepper, onion
- Fresh lime, cilantro, and naan for serving

Instructions:

1. Sauté veggies until tender.
2. Stir in curry paste, then coconut milk and chickpeas.
3. Simmer until rich and aromatic.
4. Finish with lime juice and serve with warm naan.

Capricorn Root Vegetable Tart

Ingredients:

- Puff pastry sheet
- Thinly sliced carrots, beets, parsnips, and sweet potatoes
- Herbed goat cheese or ricotta
- Olive oil, thyme, sea salt

Instructions:

1. Spread cheese on thawed pastry.
2. Arrange root slices in a spiral or rows.
3. Drizzle with oil, season, and bake at 400°F (200°C) until golden.
4. Slice and serve warm.

Aquarius Moonbeam Matcha Bowl

Ingredients:

- Greek yogurt or plant-based alternative
- Matcha powder
- Kiwi slices, blueberries, coconut flakes
- Chia seeds and puffed quinoa

Instructions:

1. Whisk matcha into yogurt until vibrant.
2. Scoop into a bowl, swirl for effect.
3. Arrange toppings in lunar alignment.
4. Chill and enjoy under starlight.

Pisces Neptune's Paella

Ingredients:

- Arborio or bomba rice
- Saffron threads, smoked paprika
- Mussels, shrimp, calamari (or vegan seafood)
- Peas, roasted red peppers, garlic, onion
- Lemon wedges

Instructions:

1. Sauté aromatics, stir in rice and spices.
2. Gradually add broth, letting flavors infuse.
3. Nestle in seafood and cook until tender.
4. Finish with peas, lemon, and a shimmer of sea salt.

Aries Bold BBQ Jackfruit

Ingredients:

- Young green jackfruit (canned, drained)
- BBQ sauce with a kick
- Smoked paprika, garlic powder
- Buns, pickled onions, slaw

Instructions:

1. Shred jackfruit and sauté with spices.
2. Simmer in BBQ sauce until sticky and bold.
3. Load onto buns with tangy slaw and pickles.
4. Serve hot with extra sass.

Taurus Rustic Olive Bread

Ingredients:

- Bread flour
- Yeast, warm water, salt
- Chopped kalamata and green olives
- Fresh rosemary

Instructions:

1. Combine ingredients into a shaggy dough.
2. Let rise until doubled.
3. Shape into a loaf, score top, and bake at 425°F (220°C) until crusty.
4. Cool and serve with good olive oil.

Gemini Two-Tone Pasta Salad

Ingredients:

- Bowtie or rotini pasta (regular and spinach)
- Cherry tomatoes, cucumber, feta
- Kalamata olives, basil
- Two dressings: balsamic glaze & lemon herb vinaigrette

Instructions:

1. Boil both pastas together or separate. Cool.
2. Toss one side with balsamic, the other with citrus.
3. Plate side by side or swirl together.
4. Garnish with basil and a playful smirk.

Cancer Creamy Clam Chowder

Ingredients:

- Clams (fresh or canned)
- Potatoes, celery, onion
- Heavy cream or coconut milk
- Butter, thyme, bay leaf
- Bacon bits (optional)

Instructions:

1. Sauté vegetables in butter.
2. Add broth and clams, simmer until tender.
3. Stir in cream and seasonings.
4. Serve warm in a sourdough bowl or deep dish, cozy and rich.

Leo Golden Mango Sorbet

Ingredients:

- 3 ripe mangoes, peeled and chopped
- Juice of 1 lime
- 1/2 cup sugar (or honey)
- 1/2 cup water
- Pinch of salt

Instructions:

1. In a saucepan, combine sugar and water. Heat until dissolved, then cool.
2. Blend mango, lime juice, syrup, and salt until smooth.
3. Chill for 2 hours, then churn in an ice cream maker or freeze in a shallow tray, stirring every 30 minutes until smooth.
4. Scoop and serve with fresh mint or chili-lime salt.

Virgo Lemon Thyme Roasted Chicken

Ingredients:

- 1 whole chicken (3–4 lbs)
- 2 lemons, halved
- 5–6 sprigs fresh thyme
- 4 garlic cloves, smashed
- Salt, pepper, olive oil

Instructions:

1. Preheat oven to 425°F (220°C).
2. Stuff chicken cavity with lemons, garlic, and thyme.
3. Rub skin with olive oil, salt, and pepper.
4. Roast for 1 hour 15 minutes or until juices run clear. Rest before carving.
5. Serve with roasted veggies or a side salad.

Libra Dual-Chocolate Fondue

Ingredients:

- 1 cup dark chocolate chips
- 1 cup white chocolate chips
- 1/2 cup heavy cream (divided)
- Fresh fruit, marshmallows, cookies for dipping

Instructions:

1. In two bowls, microwave each type of chocolate with 1/4 cup cream until melted. Stir until silky.
2. Pour side by side in a divided fondue pot or swirl together in one bowl.
3. Serve immediately with assorted dippables.

Scorpio Crimson Beet Smoothie

Ingredients:

- 1 small roasted beet, peeled
- 1 banana
- 1/2 cup frozen mixed berries
- 1/2 cup Greek yogurt
- 1/2 cup orange juice
- Honey (optional)

Instructions:

1. Blend all ingredients until creamy.
2. Taste and add honey if needed.
3. Pour into a tall glass and garnish with a berry or mint.

Sagittarius Moroccan Tagine Adventure

Ingredients:

- 1 lb chicken thighs (or chickpeas for vegetarian)
- 1 onion, sliced
- 2 cloves garlic, minced
- 1 tsp cumin, 1/2 tsp cinnamon, 1 tsp paprika
- 1 cup chopped tomatoes
- 1/2 cup dried apricots
- 1/2 cup vegetable or chicken broth
- Olive oil, salt, pepper
- Couscous for serving

Instructions:

1. Sear chicken in olive oil, remove. Sauté onion and garlic.
2. Add spices, tomatoes, apricots, and broth. Simmer.
3. Return chicken, cover, and cook until tender.
4. Serve over couscous with cilantro and lemon.

Capricorn Stone Oven Flatbread

Ingredients:

- 2 cups all-purpose flour
- 3/4 cup warm water
- 1 tsp salt
- 1 tbsp olive oil
- Optional toppings: rosemary, garlic, sea salt

Instructions:

1. Mix flour, salt, water, and oil into dough. Rest 30 min.
2. Roll thin and top as desired.
3. Bake on a hot stone or skillet at 450°F (230°C) until bubbly and golden.
4. Slice and enjoy with dips or cheese.

Aquarius Starfruit Citrus Ceviche

Ingredients:

- 1/2 lb firm white fish (or hearts of palm for vegan)
- Juice of 2 limes + 1 orange
- 1 starfruit, sliced
- 1/2 red onion, thinly sliced
- 1/2 jalapeño, minced
- Fresh cilantro, salt, pepper

Instructions:

1. Dice fish and marinate in citrus juice for 30–45 min (until opaque).
2. Drain slightly and toss with starfruit, onion, jalapeño, and herbs.
3. Chill, then serve in a chilled glass or on tostadas.

Pisces Dreamy Seafoam Cupcakes

Ingredients:

- 1 box white cake mix
- 1/2 cup milk + 1/2 cup coconut milk
- 3 egg whites
- Blue and green food coloring
- Whipped cream frosting

Instructions:

1. Prepare cake mix with milks and egg whites.
2. Divide batter and color each half. Swirl together in liners.
3. Bake per box directions.
4. Cool and frost with fluffy whipped topping. Garnish with edible pearls or sea salt.

Aries Blazing Hot Wings

Ingredients:

- 2 lbs chicken wings
- 1/2 cup hot sauce (Frank's or similar)
- 2 tbsp butter
- 1 tbsp honey
- Cayenne to taste

Instructions:

1. Bake or fry wings until crispy.
2. Melt butter with hot sauce and honey.
3. Toss wings in sauce, broil 5 minutes for extra char.
4. Serve with ranch and celery.

Pisces Floating Fish Cakes

Ingredients:

- 1/2 lb cod or white fish, cooked and flaked
- 1/2 cup mashed potatoes
- 1 egg
- 1/4 cup breadcrumbs
- Green onion, lemon zest, salt, pepper

Instructions:

1. Mix ingredients and shape into small cakes.
2. Chill 15 minutes.
3. Pan-fry in olive oil until golden on each side.
4. Serve with lemon aioli or dill sauce.

www.ingramcontent.com/pod-product-compliance
Lightning Source LLC
LaVergne TN
LVHW081330060526
838201LV00055B/2548